Internet DOs & DON'Ts

Be Nice Online

Shannon Miller

PowerKiDS press.

New York

Published in 2014 by The Rosen Publishing Group, Inc.
29 East 21st Street, New York, NY 10010

First Edition

Editor: Jennifer Way
Book Design: Andrew Povolny

Photo Credits: Cover Derek E. Rothchild/The Image Bank/Getty Images; p. 5 Pixland/Thinkstock; p. 7 Jupiter Images/Brand X Pictures/Thinkstock; p. 9 Moodboard/Cultura/Getty Images; p. 11 Stockbyte/Thinkstock; p. 13 Evan Sklar/Botanica/Getty Images; p. 15 quavondo/E+/Getty Images; p. 17 Jose Luis Pelaez Inc./Blend Images/Getty Images; p. 19 SW Productions/Photodisc/Getty Images; p. 21 Jupiter Images/Comstock/Thinkstock; p. 23 Monkey Business/Thinkstock.

Library of Congress Cataloging-in-Publication Data

Miller, Shannon.
 Be nice online / by Shannon Miller. – First edition.
     pages cm. — (Internet dos & don'ts)
 Includes index.
 ISBN 978-1-4777-0756-2 (library binding) — ISBN 978-1-4777-1566-6 (pbk.) —
 ISBN 978-1-4777-1567-3 (6-pack)
 1. Internet and children—Juvenile literature. 2. Online etiquette—Juvenile literature. 3. Cyberbullying—Prevention—Juvenile literature. I. Title.
 HQ784.I58M549 2014
 004.67'8083—dc23
                              2013000195

Manufactured in the United States of America

CPSIA Compliance Information: Batch #S13PK4: For Further Information contact Rosen Publishing, New York, New York at 1-800-237-9932

Contents

You can work on projects online. You can email and **chat** with friends. You can also talk to people using tools like Skype. It is important to be nice. This book will tell you why.

5

Being nice is thinking about others' feelings. Other people should think about your feelings as well. You feel sad or angry sometimes. Other people also have these feelings.

It is not right to make someone feel bad. It is wrong even if you are angry with her. Never say things to make someone feel bad.

9

You may make a friend feel bad by mistake. Everyone makes mistakes. Say you are sorry if this happens.

Stop and think before you type. Calm down if you are angry. This will stop you from saying mean things. Always use kind and friendly words online.

13

Do not share secrets online. It is hard to erase something once it is sent or posted. A secret may not stay secret!

Do not share **private** facts about yourself. Do not share private facts about others. Sharing these facts can cause trouble.

People should be nice to you online. Sometimes this does not happen. Someone may **bully** you. Do not say something mean back. The bully wants to know he hurt your feelings.

Tell the bully to leave you alone.
Tell an adult if you are bullied.
She will help you. She can help
make the bully stop.

Everyone has the right to feel safe online. No one has the right to make others feel bad. Be nice online. That is a big **Internet** do!

23

WORDS TO KNOW

bully (BUL-ee) A person who uses hurtful words or actions toward others.

chat (CHAT) Using a computer to "talk" to another person.

Internet (IN-ter-net) A network that connects computers around the world. The Internet provides facts and information.

private (PRY-vit) Not meant for strangers to know.

INDEX

WEBSITES

Due to the changing nature of Internet links, PowerKids Press has developed an online list of websites related to the subject of this book. This site is updated regularly. Please use this link to access the list:
www.powerkidslinks.com/idd/nice/